HEINEMANN Profiles

Henry Ford

John Malam

First published in Great Britain by Heinemann Library, Halley Court, Jordan Hill, Oxford OX2 8EJ, a division of Reed Educational and Professional Publishing Ltd.
Heinemann is a registered trademark of Reed Educational & Professional Publishing Limited.

OXFORD MELBOURNE AUCKLAND JOHANNESBURG BLANTYRE GABORONE IBADAN PORTSMOUTH NH (USA) CHICAGO

Produced for Heinemann Library by Discovery Books Limited
Edited by Rosemary Williams
Designed by Ian Winton
Originated by Dot Gradations
Printed and bound in Hong Kong/China

ISBN 0 431 08642 7

05 04 03 02 01
10 9 8 7 6 5 4 3 2 1

British Library Cataloguing in Publication Data

Malam, John
Henry Ford. – (Heinemann Profiles)
1. Ford, Henry, 1863-1947 – Juvenile literature 2. Ford Motor Company – Juvenile literature 3. Industrialists – United States – Biography – Juvenile literature 4. Motor vehicle industry – United States – Biography – Juvenile literature
I. Title
338.7'629222'092

Acknowledgements
The Publishers would like to thank the following for permission to reproduce photographs: p14 Science Museum/Science & Society Picture Library, p25 Peter Newark's American Pictures, p26 Bettman/Corbis

All other photographs reproduced from the collections of the Henry Ford Museum & Greenfield Village and from Ford Motor Company, UK.

Every effort has been made to contact copyright holders of any material reproduced in this book. Any omissions will be rectified in subsequent printings if notice is given to the Publisher.

Any words appearing in the text in bold, **like this**, are explained in the Glossary.

Contents

Who Was Henry Ford?

As we look back through the centuries, very few people can claim to have changed the world in which we live today. Yet in the area of transport, one person has influenced the lives of millions of people. His name was Henry Ford, and this is his story.

Of the many machines which help us to travel, it is the motor car that has given us the freedom to cross land quickly, cheaply, safely and in comfort. Invented in the 19th century, the motor car revolutionized personal and public transport in the 20th century, and Henry Ford, more than any other person, was the leader of that revolution.

Henry Ford (1863-1947), engineer and pioneer car manufacturer. The first official Ford Motor Company portrait in 1904.

Birth of the motor car

Henry Ford was not the inventor of the motor car. In 1886, Karl Benz (1844–1929), a German **engineer**, **registered** a design for a three-wheeled vehicle. Although motor vehicles had been built before this date, it was Benz's design which proved to be the best. The motor car was born, and with it came the beginnings of an industry upon which Henry Ford was to build his reputation.

Ford cars were among the first mass produced motor vehicles in the world.

A GRAND IDEA

From simple beginnings as a farm boy in Michigan, USA, Henry Ford grew to become one of the world's wealthiest people. He was not to be a humble farmer like his ancestors. Instead, his **destiny** lay in the new **technology** of his day – the motor car – and in a grand idea: he wanted to build cars that ordinary people could afford.

Ford sensed that the motor car would change people's lives for the better, and for that to happen he knew he had to find a way of building cars quickly and cheaply. That meant changing the way in which **manufacturing industry** worked.

What Ford created was far more than a cheap car for the masses – he **transformed** the **fledgling motor car industry** from backyard workshops into an international business success. His Ford Motor Company, established in 1903, is one of today's leading car manufacturers.

Farewell Ireland, Hello America

Henry Ford's story begins not in America but in Ireland, where the Ford family had its roots. In the first half of the 1800s the Fords were farmers at Ballinascarty, County Cork. It was here that Henry Ford's grandfather, John Ford, worked. Life was hard for the farmers of Ireland, but in the 1840s a disaster struck them. In 1846, blight (a fungus) attacked their potato crops, one of their main sources of nutrition. Once infected, nothing could be done to save the plants, which rotted in the fields. The outbreak lasted three years and thousands of Irish families were forced to leave the land, or face starvation. Known as the Great Famine, it was a time of poverty and hardship.

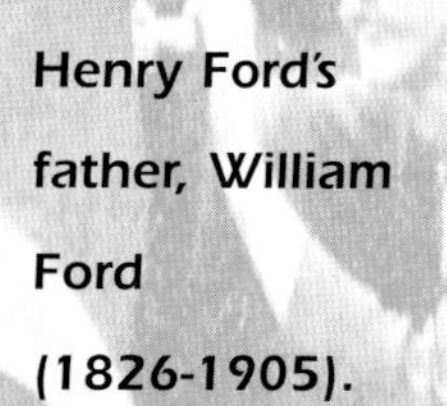

Henry Ford's father, William Ford (1826-1905).

Among the people affected by the famine were John Ford and his family. They decided to **emigrate** to America to begin a new, and hopefully better, life. And so, in 1847, John Ford, his elderly mother, his wife, Thomasina, and their seven children went to Cork, the nearest seaport on the Atlantic coast, and boarded an emigration ship.

The clapboard farmhouse at Dearborn, Michigan, where Henry Ford was born.

A new home

The Fords sailed to Canada, from where they travelled south into the United States of America, reaching the state of Michigan in 1848. At the settlement of Dearbornville (which later became Dearborn) the family bought land and set about making a clearing in the wildwood.

Henry Ford is born

The Ford family settled down. In 1861, John Ford's son, William, married Mary Litogot, the foster daughter of a neighbouring family. William was 35, Mary was 22. On the morning of 30 July 1863, Mary gave birth to a son in their Dearborn farmhouse. They named him Henry. He was born during the **American Civil War** (1861-65), when the country was torn apart by a conflict that changed its future. Henry would one day change the course of his country's future, too.

> 'The first thing I remember in my life is my father taking my brother and myself to see a bird's nest ... I remember the nest with four eggs and also the bird and hearing it sing.'
>
> Henry Ford's earliest memory, aged about three years old

Raised on a Farm

Henry Ford spent his childhood years on his parents' 90-acre farm, where wheat, oats, apples and peaches were grown, and cows, pigs and sheep were raised. As the eldest child (he had three brothers and two sisters), Henry was expected to help on the farm. But he showed little interest in the work, and would refuse to do a job if he felt like it. A stubborn and rebellious child, Henry preferred the excitement of Detroit during the family's shopping trips there, with all the din of the riverfront machinery.

'... considering the results, there was too much work on the place.'

Henry Ford's recollections of life on his father's farm

An interest in mechanics

When Henry was seven he went to Dearborn's only school, where he showed a talent for mathematics, but not for English. Another talent was emerging as well: he was starting to show an interest in machines. He became fascinated by clocks and watches. With a set of tiny tools he'd made himself he learnt how to take their complicated **mechanisms** apart, fix them if they were broken, then reassemble them. His mother called him 'her born mechanic'.

'Machines are to a mechanic what books are to a writer. He gets ideas from them, and if he has any brains, he applies those ideas.'

Henry Ford

1876 – GRIEF AND INSPIRATION

Two events occurred in 1876 that influenced the teenage Ford. In March his beloved mother died. Her death was a great blow to him. For the rest of his life Henry remembered the lessons she had taught him: it was his mother who had encouraged him never to give up, never to pity himself if things went wrong, and to show patience and courage when doing jobs he might not like. In old age, when asked to explain his business success, Henry replied: 'I have tried to live my life as my mother would have wished.'

The second major event of 1876 came in mid-summer, when he saw a **steam engine** moving under its own power along a dirt road. It was the first time Henry had seen a vehicle moving without the aid of horses to pull it – and the experience filled his young head with ideas. When, years later, he recalled that July day, he said: '... it was that engine which took me into **automotive transportation**.'

Henry Ford's mother, Mary Litogot Ford (1839-76).

Starting Work

'**Automotive transportation**', as Henry referred to it, was the dream of many **engineers**. The 19th century had already given rise to the steam locomotive, the steam ship and the bicycle. Also, inventors in Belgium, France and Germany had begun to experiment in building '**horseless carriages**'. The French had a word for them – '**automobiles**'.

Henry Ford, aged about seventeen, when he was an apprentice engineer in Detroit.

It was against this background of progress in transport and **technology** that Henry Ford's future developed. The late 1800s were a time of quickening **industrialization** in America and Europe, and Ford had every intention of becoming involved with the opportunities the **era** offered.

His mind was made up: he would leave school as soon as he could and train to be an engineer.

In December 1879, sixteen-year-old Henry left the family farm at Dearborn and walked the 14 kilometres (9 miles) to the industrial city of Detroit, to begin work at the engineering firm of James F Flower & Brothers.

A HEAD FOR BUSINESS

It took several years to train as an engineer, which seemed forever to Henry. Not content with staying long in any one job, he moved to other firms in Detroit so that he could learn more about engineering. As an **apprentice** he earned little money, so in the evenings he worked as a watch-repairer. This gave him the idea of starting up his own watch-making business, but the difference would be that Henry wanted to make watches that everyone could afford. When he estimated that to make a watch that would sell for as little as 30 cents, he would need to produce 2000 a day – more than half a million a year – he soon gave up the idea. How could he possibly hope to sell so many watches? He was not yet twenty, but he had already started to think about **mass production**, an entirely new method of working.

> 'In the long run, people are going to buy the cheapest and best article – no matter where it's made.'
>
> Henry Ford

Back on the Farm

With his **apprenticeship** over, Henry could call himself an **engineer**. However, instead of looking for a job in Detroit, he returned to Dearborn and the family farm. In the peace of the countryside he could think about his future, and how he could put his new-found engineering knowledge to good use. It wasn't long before his skill with machinery was called upon.

A neighbour had bought a small **steam engine** to help in jobs around his farm. It could do the work of several men and horses, and Henry learned how it worked and how to operate it. The summer of 1882 was a happy one as he travelled from farm to farm taking the portable steam engine to help his neighbours.

A family man

Henry Ford met Clara Bryant, his future wife, on New Year's Day, 1885. He fell in love with her immediately. Clara was eighteen and he made little impression on her then, but when they met again a whole year later, she found that Henry was not like the other young men of the area. They were interested in everyday things, but Henry Ford was a sensible, serious-minded fellow with lots of practical ideas – and Clara grew to like him.

Henry's father, William, must have thought his son had returned to Dearborn to settle down as a farmer. In 1886, William gave Henry 80 acres of uncleared woodland for himself. Henry could fell the trees, clear the land and farm it. His beloved steam engines would make the hard work so much easier. History would be very different if Henry had become a farmer, but this was never going to be the life for him.

Clara Bryant Ford in 1888.

Henry and Clara were married on 11 April 1888. Henry was almost 25. Clara came from a farming family, and probably thought she was marrying a farmer. But with his interest in machines and **technology**, Henry Ford was no ordinary farmer. He must have seemed a very 'modern man'.

The engine that sparked an idea

Time and again Henry was called away from the farm to repair **steam engines**. And then, on a trip to a Detroit factory, he saw a new type of engine that had been invented by a German **engineer**, Nikolaus August Otto (1832–91). Powered by petrol, not steam, it was an **internal combustion engine** and it made its power from gas expanding inside a **cylinder**.

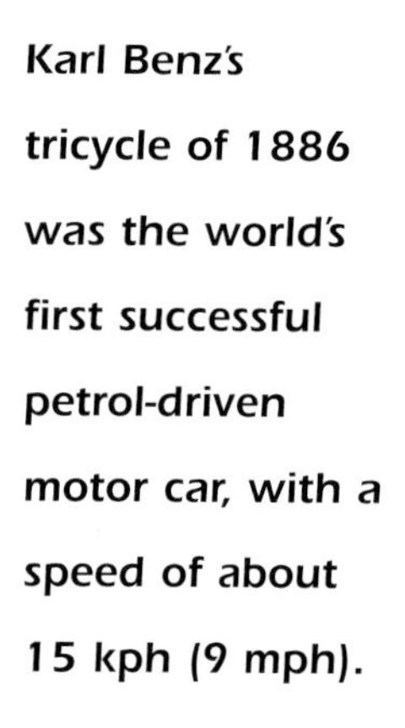

Karl Benz's tricycle of 1886 was the world's first successful petrol-driven motor car, with a speed of about 15 kph (9 mph).

The new engine was smaller and lighter than the steam engines Henry was used to, and it also needed **electricity**, which he knew little about. Back home in Dearborn, Henry explained to Clara what he had seen. He wondered if it would be possible to mount the internal combustion engine on wheels, and use it to move a vehicle along. Henry had to find out –

Henry Ford (circled) with fellow workers in the engine room of the Edison Illuminating Company, Detroit, about 1895.

but first he had to learn about electricity, and that meant leaving the farm and moving to Detroit where, in 1891, Henry began working for the Edison Illuminating Company. Here he learnt about electricity, and from then on Henry's life with '**automotive transportation**' began a new chapter.

The light of the future

In 1890s America, the Edison Illuminating Company was one of the most modern businesses in the land. Just twelve years before Henry Ford joined the firm, its founder, Thomas Edison (1847-1931), had made one of the greatest breakthroughs in the history of science when in 1879 he had invented the electric light bulb. Detroit's homes, businesses and streets were lit with the 'light of the future'.

1896 – A Car Is Born

One year stands out as a **milestone** in the life of Henry Ford. That year was 1896, and it has gone down in history as the year the first Ford motor car was built.

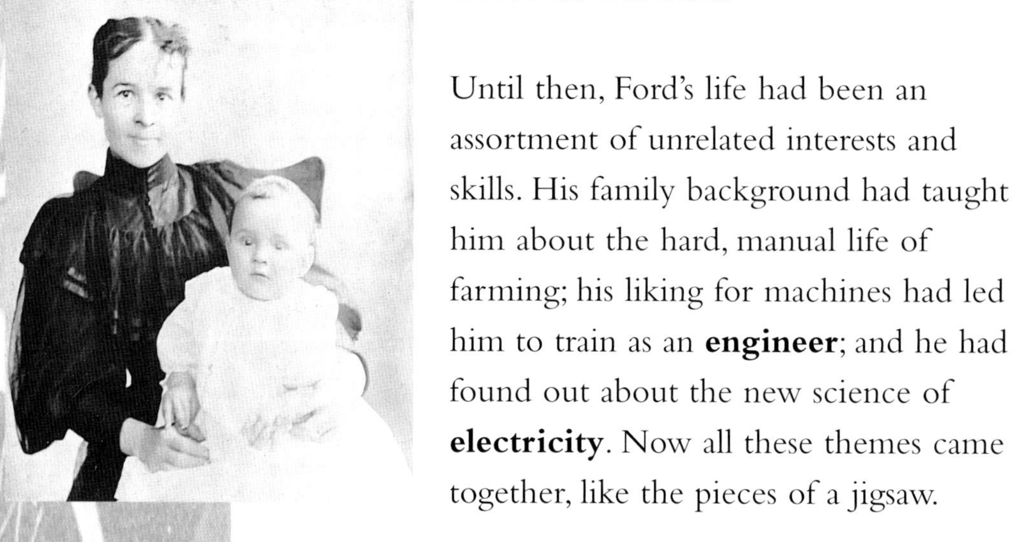

Until then, Ford's life had been an assortment of unrelated interests and skills. His family background had taught him about the hard, manual life of farming; his liking for machines had led him to train as an **engineer**; and he had found out about the new science of **electricity**. Now all these themes came together, like the pieces of a jigsaw.

Clara, in 1894, with their only child, Edsel Ford (1893-1943).

Workshops at work and home

As chief engineer for the Edison Illuminating Company, Ford had a good job in a new industry. It brought him into contact with other like-minded engineers – men who felt that the new **technology** of the day could be used to bring about great changes.

At work, Ford had his own private workshop. It was here in the early 1890s that he began his experiments in building petrol-driven **internal combustion engines**. Ford's plan was to make a vehicle for the road. He transferred his experiments to the family home at 58 Bagley Avenue, Detroit. Here, at the back of the house was a small brick outbuilding, a former coalshed, which became the centre of his car-making activities. Ford did not work alone in his home workshop – far from it. He was helped by friends and colleagues who shared his vision of the future, each of whom brought skills in such areas as metal-working, electricity and **fuel supply** to the project. Another important member of the team was Clara Ford, whom Henry affectionately called 'The Believer'. She took his ideas seriously, certain he was about to invent something sensational. When asked by visitors what he was working on, she replied: 'Henry is making something, and maybe some day I'll tell you.'

A reconstruction of Ford's workshop at 58 Bagley Avenue, Detroit, viewed from the wall he partly demolished.

When he was older, Ford would recall his early days with motor cars, when he said he had a vision of the future: '[I dreamed of making] some kind of a light steam car that would take the place of horses … especially as a tractor to attend to the excessively hard labour of ploughing. It occurred to me … that precisely the same idea might be applied to a carriage or wagon on the road … but the idea of the carriage at first did not seem so practical to me as the idea of an engine to do the harder farm work.'

The Quadricycle

In 1896, after almost three years of work, the vehicle created in the Bagley Avenue workshop was finally finished. They called it the Quadricycle because it looked like two bicycles side by side. Just imagine the excitement the team must have felt. Even though it was the middle of the night, they were tired and outside it was pouring with rain – they just wanted to find out straight away if their motor car would work.

Ford driving the Quadricycle in 1896. He became known as 'Crazy Ford' in Detroit.

But the Quadricycle turned out to be too big to go through the door. And so, at about 3 am on the morning of 4 June 1896, Henry Ford took an axe and knocked down

Quadricycle facts

Maximum power	4 hp (horse power) – many modern cars have about 100 hp
Length	1.95 m (6ft 5in)
Top speed	32 kph (20 mph)
Brakes	none
Weight	226 kg (500 lb)

part of the wall of the workshop. Hearing the commotion, Clara rushed outside. The petrol engine was started, Ford climbed into the saddle, held on to the **steering tiller** and drove out into the night's rain.

Ford took the Quadricycle for a test drive, moving slowly along the streets of Detroit. Jim Bishop, one of the **engineers** who had helped build the car, escorted the noisy vehicle, riding ahead of it on a bicycle.

Towards the end of 1896, Ford was introduced to his hero, Thomas Edison, the great inventor and founder of the Edison Illuminating Company, for whom Ford still worked. It was a turning point in Ford's life. Edison was impressed with Ford's petrol-driven car, saying: 'Young man, that's the thing! Your car is self-contained – it carries its own powerplant – no fire, no boiler, no smoke, no steam. You have the thing. Keep at it!'

Ford Goes into Business

Ford's thoughts turned towards making cars by the hundred. He was sure it could be done, and, importantly, he was convinced the public would buy them. But to do that meant setting up a company, and that needed a lot of money – which Ford didn't have.

After driving the Quadricycle for 1600 kilometres (1000 miles), Ford sold it for $200 to Charles Ainsley – the first-ever customer for a Ford motor car. Ford had not built the Quadricycle to sell. Instead, he had built it as an **experimental vehicle** to test his ideas for making cars, but the money from the sale helped Ford to plan his next venture.

The Detroit Automobile Company: 1899 to 1900

Henry Ford was not the only person in America who wanted to create a successful car-making business. By 1899 there were already 80 factories across the country making cars: other people had seen the future too.

Ford now faced a difficult decision, especially as he had a family to support. 'I had to choose between my job and my **automobile**,' he said later. He chose his automobile, and in July of that year Ford went into **partnership** with several wealthy local businessmen. It was their money that led to the founding of the Detroit Automobile Company. Ford resigned from the Edison Illuminating Company and went to work full-time at the new car firm, taking a risky cut in salary. His job was to oversee the production of the company's car – whatever it was to be.

The plan was to have the first cars ready for sale by October 1899 – just three months after the company had been set up. But this never happened because Ford, although a **genius**, had a lot to learn about working with other people. Convinced that he was always right, he wouldn't listen to the advice of his business partners and employees, with the result that fewer than twelve vehicles were made in fifteen months.

As it was losing money for its owners, the company was closed down in November 1900, and its materials, parts and equipment were sold for scrap. Henry was sacked by his partners at a meeting he could not bring himself to attend. 'If they ask for me,' he told a colleague, 'tell them I have gone out of town.' Without a job, Henry could no longer afford to keep a home, and the family had to go and live with Henry's father, now retired, in Detroit.

The Henry Ford Company: 1901 to 1902

But Ford soon found other businessmen to support him financially, and another new company was set up. It was called the Henry Ford Company, and Ford was its chief **engineer**. The owners thought they were in business to make small cars, but, determined as ever, Ford had a very different idea.

He intended to make racing cars. The owners were furious, and a few months later Ford was paid $900 to leave the company that bore his name. Its owners continued without him, with great success. They

Some of Henry Ford's original backers, with Ford and one of his early cars.

Henry Ford at the wheel of the first Ford racer, with Spider Huff on the running board, in 1901, the year Ford became the American motor racing champion.

changed the company name to the Cadillac **Automobile** Company. (Today, this company is part of General Motors, the world's largest car-maker.)

Ford's dismissal

Years later, in Henry's rather different version of events about being sacked from the Henry Ford Company, he said that it was the directors who had wanted him to build racing cars, whereas he himself had only been interested in building popular, low-priced cars.

Success, at Last!

The failure of the Detroit **Automobile** Company, followed by his departure from the Henry Ford Company, didn't put Ford off the idea of one day having his own car-making business. But until then, Ford pursued his new interest in racing cars.

A race to the future

The first years of the 1900s welcomed the dawning of an age of peace, prosperity and progress. A new sport was born at around this time, too – motor racing. The question everyone was asking was: 'How fast can a car go?'

The public were fascinated by the sight of cars racing at speeds approaching 65 kph (40 mph). Ford saw this as his opportunity to return to car-making. With money from yet another new **backer**, Ford built two racers, both 3 metres (10 feet) in length. One, called Arrow, was painted yellow. The other, called 999, was red. Both were named after high-speed American steam locomotives. Despite the fact that Henry had never raced before, he drove the Arrow in a 1901 race against the leading American car-maker Alexander Winton, watched by a crowd of 8000. 'The people went wild,' Clara remembered, as Ford's racer roared home the winner.

'The roar of those cylinders at full speed was enough to half kill a man,' said Henry. 'Going over Niagara Falls would have been a pastime after a ride in the 999.'

Of the two racers, the 999 was chosen to enter a race over 8 kilometres (5 miles), with cars entered by several American car-makers.

In October 1902, Ford's 999 racer, driven by Barney Oldfield, a former racing cyclist, set a new American land-speed record of 5 minutes 28 seconds for the distance – a little more than a minute a mile (1.6 kilometres).

Barney Oldfield winning in the 999 racer, in 1902. Painted by H C McBarron.

The Ford Motor Company: 1903 to the present day

Between 1902 and 1908, no fewer than 502 companies were formed in America to build cars. Yet again, Ford found himself searching for a wealthy **backer** to set him up in business. Without financial help, Ford's ideas would come to nothing.

INCORPORATED UNDER THE LAWS OF THE STATE OF MICHIGAN

NUMBER

SHARES 255

FORD MOTOR COMPANY.

CAPITAL $150,000.

FULLY PAID. NON-ASSESSABLE.

THIS CERTIFIES THAT Henry Ford is the owner of Two Hundred and Fifty Five Shares of the Capital Stock of FORD MOTOR COMPANY, transferable only on the books of the Corporation by the holder hereof in person or by Attorney upon surrender of this Certificate properly endorsed.

In Witness Whereof, the said Corporation has caused this Certificate to be signed by its duly authorized officers and to be sealed with the Seal of the Corporation this [illegible] day of June A.D. 1903

Shares $100 Each.

The original share certificate for Henry Ford's initial investment in his motor company.

Not for the first time (and despite a reputation for arrogance and stubbornness), Ford was in luck. In 1902, a rich coal merchant from Detroit, Alex Malcomson, went into **partnership** with Ford. The plan was to build a passenger car, and the result was a vehicle known simply as the Ford Model A. Although it looked just like the cars being made by many other makers, its appearance was deceptive. Using his knowledge of racing cars, Ford and his team had found a way of improving the Model A's engine. It was more powerful than other cars, and it marked a turning point for Henry Ford. On 16 June 1903, Ford, Malcomson and their partners established the Ford Motor Company. The car they pinned their hopes on was the Ford Model A.

The Ford Model A. The upholstered rear seat shown here was an optional extra that converted the car to a four-seater model.

If it was a success, perhaps the new company stood a chance of not only surviving, but of emerging as America's leading car-maker.

'The most perfect machine on the market'

The Ford Model A was indeed a success. In July 1903, Dr E Pfennig, a dentist from Chicago, became the first customer of the Ford Motor Company when he bought a Ford Model A. It cost him $850. The Ford Model A was sold as 'the most perfect machine on the market', and orders came to the Detroit factory from all over the United States. Within eight months, 658 had been sold, and by the end of 1904 the company's **output** had reached 1700 vehicles. Henry Ford had found success as a car-maker at last.

Making a Car, the Early Method

A car factory today is a highly **automated** place of work. Cars are built inside clean, well-lit buildings, where **conveyor belts** and trackways move car parts along at a steady rate, to be assembled by computerized machines, and also by human workers. This is very different from car factories of a century ago, like the ones where the first Fords were made.

When cars were built by hand

Like many other **manufacturing industries** of the time – such as those that made bicycles, locomotives and ships – car-makers built their vehicles by hand, one at a time. In the beginning the Ford Motor Company worked this way too. The basic component was the car **chassis**, which usually stood on one spot until the car was finished. Parts were carried to the chassis to be fixed in place, like assembling a giant three-dimensional jigsaw. After painting and

Notable Fords: 1903 to 1908

Early Ford cars were named after letters of the alphabet (some experimental models never reached the production stage).

Ford	US price	Top speed	Date
Model A	$850	48 kph (30 mph)	1903
Model B	$2000	64 kph (40 mph)	1904
Model C	$1000	61 kph (38 mph)	1904
Model F	$1200	56 kph (35 mph)	1905
Model K	$2500–$2800	96 kph (60 mph)	1905
Model N	$600	72 kph (45 mph)	1905
Model R	$750	72 kph (45 mph)	1907
Model S	$700	72 kph (45 mph)	1907
Model T	$260–$850	67 kph (42 mph)	1908

Clara Ford driving a Model N past the Ford Motor Company's Piquette Avenue plant in 1905.

upholstering, the car was finished and was ready for sale.

An inefficient method

Even after cars were assembled on stands that could be moved from one team of workers to the next, the process was still time consuming and therefore expensive. If Henry Ford's grand idea of building cars that ordinary people could afford was ever going to happen, then a new method of making cars was essential.

Henry Ford with his son, Edsel, aged 12, aboard a Model F in 1905.

Glory Days – the Model T Story

Of all the different cars built by Henry Ford, one has become legendary. This was the Ford Model T, and it was this car more than any other that fulfilled Ford's dream of building a car that ordinary people could afford. It revolutionized the motor industry, not only in America, but in Europe, too.

A 1910 Model T. By 1914 the Model T, in the interests of streamlining the production process, was no longer available in red, blue, green or grey, but you could have 'any colour so long as it is black'.

For Henry Ford, the early years of the Ford Motor Company were like a voyage of discovery, but his method of working by instinct frustrated his colleagues. Unable to read an engineering drawing, Henry preferred to hold a part in his hands to tell if it was well designed! Some of the cars the company built between 1903 and 1908 were successful (such as the Ford Model A), but others were not. The expensive Ford Model K sold at a loss, and almost put the company out of business.

But with each new model built, Ford was trying to improve on the preceding one. Learning both from his successes and his failures, Ford was moving ever closer to making a world-class car.

A new metal from Europe

Henry Ford learnt from other car-makers, too. In 1905 he was at a race meeting at which a car from a French company crashed. Pieces of its steel were strewn across the racetrack. Ford picked a piece up. It was lighter and stronger than the metal used to build his cars – and he wanted it. 'That is the kind of material we ought to have in our cars,' he said.

Ford found an American company to make the lightweight metal (called **vanadium steel**), and in 1907 he began using it for his cars, starting with the Ford Model N. The new steel improved the quality of Ford cars, making them lighter and stronger than before. But Ford felt he could make things even better – he wanted to make a car that was lightweight, strong, reliable and, most of all, inexpensive to buy.

> 'I will build a motor car for the great multitude. It will be large enough for the family but small enough for the individual to run and care for. It will be constructed of the best materials... it will be so low in price that no man making a good salary will be unable to own one.'
>
> Henry Ford describing his vision of a 'dream car', in 1907

'A motor car for the great multitude'

For an entire year Ford and his team of **designers** and **engineers** planned the new car. Called the Ford Model T, it was to be made from **vanadium steel**. The project was complicated and the team found themselves doing things no other car-makers had even attempted before. Ford brought his mother's old rocking chair from the farmhouse, and he sat with the engineers as they worked. Some of the team thought the car might not stand up to everyday use, but Ford was convinced it would. A tough man to work for, Ford inspected every detail of the new design, insisting on getting small things absolutely right. He was determined to create the world's best car.

'It plowed the field
that afternoon,
And when the job
was through
It hummed a pleasant
little tune
And churned the
butter, too.'
Part of a 1917 verse on
the multiple uses of a
Ford Model T engine

A record-breaker

The first Ford Model T was sold in 1908, priced at $850 – as much as a teacher in America earned in a year then. Twelve months later 10,000 Model Ts had been sold, and the price came tumbling down. In 1916 it cost $345, and by 1925 just $260 – a price within the reach of most working people. But Henry had built far more than just an affordable car. Most roads outside towns and cities at that time were rough and unsurfaced. Breakdowns were inconvenient and expensive. Henry made sure that the Model T was a rugged car that could not only cope with such conditions better than any other car, but could even drive over dug-up fields and double as a tractor. Its simple engine design meant that a farmer, or anyone else with basic mechanical knowledge, could repair it easily.

The Ford Model T broke many records. By the time the last one rolled off the production line in December 1927, some 16.5 million 'Tin Lizzies', as they were affectionately known, had been made. Less affectionate nicknames included the 'Galloping Snail' and the 'Detroit Disaster'.

In the early 1920s, Model Ts were also made in England (at Ford's Manchester factory), Ireland, France, Spain, Italy, Germany, Denmark and Belgium. Henry Ford had put the world on wheels with a car that was described as 'useful as a pair of shoes'.

The Ford Model T was a 'universal car' that could be adapted to suit many different purposes, like the 'Ford Express', shown here around 1911.

Mass Production

Women assembling magnetos in a Ford factory in 1913. Female factory workers did not receive the $5 per day minimum wage until 1916.

A story was told about a worker at the Ford factory in Detroit: he dropped his **wrench**, and by the time he'd picked it up he was sixteen cars behind! It was only a joke – and Henry Ford, always fond of a good joke himself, repeated it on a visit to the White House to meet President Woodrow Wilson – but it makes the point about how fast the Model T car-makers worked. The 'Tin Lizzie' was the end result of a method of working called **mass production**, which enabled Henry Ford to make so many cars, so quickly and so cheaply.

The assembly line

Ford made two key changes inside his Detroit factory. First, he saved money by making many of the car parts at the factory, instead of paying high prices to buy them from other companies. Second, Ford introduced the moving **assembly line**. Instead of workers walking from car to car, the partially assembled cars were brought to them.

'Every time I reduce the charge for our car by one dollar, I get a thousand new buyers.'
Henry Ford

They stood at work benches as cars and parts moved along in front of them on chains and **conveyor belts**.

Each worker did one specific job. As Henry Ford said: 'The man who puts in a bolt does not put on the nut; the man who puts on the nut does not tighten it.' It was like assembling identical kits from the 5,000 pieces that went into making every Ford car. It was repetitive, dull work, but in 1914, to attract new workers and prevent others from quitting their jobs, Ford doubled the daily minimum wage. The '$5 day' for unskilled work was a fortune at that time, and once more Henry Ford made history. Before the assembly-line method was introduced, it had taken 12 hours to build one Ford Model T. But with mass production as many as 8000 Model Ts a day could be made.

Using the assembly-line method, a new Model T left the factory every 10 seconds.

FORD THE IDEALIST

Fair Lane, Henry Ford's 56-room mansion by the Rouge River at Dearborn, Michigan. The house was built around 1915.

The worldwide success of the Ford Model T and the use of **mass production** had helped make Henry Ford into one of the world's richest, and best-known, people. Other businessmen would have been more than satisfied to have achieved so much in so little time. But not Ford: he was restless, and was always looking for new ways to expand his business.

Ford's methods of making inexpensive cars brought him much more than wealth – he became a celebrity with the power to influence the lives of ordinary people, not just in America but in Europe, too. In 1912, Ford visited his car factories in

England and France, and for the first time saw how much in demand his cars were in Europe. He saw something else there, too. To an **astute** person like Ford, the rise of **nationalism** and the build-up of arms suggested that the nations of Europe might be on the brink of going to war with each other, and if that happened his business would suffer. What could he do to protect it?

Henry Ford realized the importance of Europe as the largest market for cars outside the USA.

THE 'PEACE SHIP'

Ford returned to America, determined to find a way of preventing a war in Europe from harming his business empire. When the **First World War** (also called the Great War) began in 1914, Ford knew he had to act. In 1915 he declared that he was ready to pay for a 'worldwide campaign for universal peace'. How he intended to organize such a grand scheme was another matter – he hadn't worked that out. Henry Ford's idea of making 'universal peace' made news headlines, and peace campaigners made contact with him, wondering how they could all work together. At a meeting someone suggested sailing a

Henry Ford (centre) on board the 'Peace Ship' as it leaves in 1915 for the ill-fated peace mission.

'Peace Ship' to Europe. Ford liked the idea, since it would gain a huge amount of **publicity** for his cause, for himself, and also for his car-making business.

Ford chartered a ship, the *King Oscar II*, which was due to sail from New York to Norway in December 1915. In a moment of rashness Ford said: 'We'll get the boys in the trenches home by Christmas.' It was an incredible thing for anyone to say, let alone an American, since the United States was not even in the war in 1915. An American newspaper printed this headline on its front page: 'Great War Ends Christmas Day: Ford to Stop It'. Another said that Ford was 'God's Fool'.

As Ford sailed on the *King Oscar II* to Norway, he started having doubts about the wisdom of his mission. The papers were making fun of him and politicians – including the president of the USA – refused to listen to him. And so, as soon as the so-called 'Peace Ship' reached Norway, Ford abandoned his plan and boarded the next ship straight back to America.

The First World War didn't end at Christmas 1915, but continued until November 1918, by which time America had become involved, and Henry Ford's car factories had been given over to making vehicles for the **war effort**.

Ford the Would-be Politician

One of Ford's 1918 campaign posters. Henry hoped he would win the votes of working people because of the freedom the motor car had given them.

Despite his great wealth – he was America's first billionaire – money never mattered that much to Henry Ford. According to a story, Ford's wife, Clara, once found a cheque for $75,000 in his pocket. He'd simply forgotten all about it. What mattered more to Ford than money was the power to influence people. His 'Peace Ship' mission had been an attempt at using the power he thought he had, but it had ended in bitter failure.

Ford was not a man to give up easily. He considered other ways to put his power to use, and in 1918 announced that he would be standing for election to the United States **Senate** from Michigan.

'Henry for Senator'

Ford had no real experience of **politics**. He was, after all, a middle-aged wealthy businessman who had spent his working life building up a car-making business. But, as the man who had made cars affordable to all, he was one of the best-known people in America. It was this popularity that he hoped would see him elected as a United States senator.

At first, things went well for Henry Ford. Farmers, who loved the freedom his cars had brought them, voted for him. Others supported him because of his wartime stand for peace. However, politics is full of traps – and there was danger ahead for Ford.

His opponents ridiculed him for his failed 'Peace Ship' mission. Then his son, Edsel, was dragged into the political campaign. Old enough to fight during the war, Edsel had avoided it, encouraged by his father. Ford's political enemies accused Edsel of **'draft dodging'** – their way of calling him a coward.

A BAD LOSER

Ford's political fate lay in the hands of the voters. It was a close contest, and the votes were counted twice. Ford lost by a narrow margin – and he was angry. He accused his opponent, Truman Newberry, of cheating. Ford claimed that Newberry had spent more money on his **election campaign** than was allowed under the rules, and, worst of all, he said Newberry was controlled by an 'influential gang of Jews'. This **racist** remark revealed a side of Ford's character that few had known before.

Ford the Extremist

Two things happened to Henry Ford in November 1918: he failed in his attempt to be elected to the United States **Senate**, and he bought himself a newspaper company. As a senator, Ford would have represented the people who had voted for him. He would have been their 'official voice' in public, and his thoughts and opinions would have been reported in newspapers and on radio stations all across America. But because Ford failed to be elected, he looked for another way to make himself heard.

A front page of the *Dearborn Independent*, 6 August 1921. The central headline betrays Ford's racist opinions.

The Ford International Weekly
THE DEARBORN INDEPENDENT
By the Year $1.50 — Dearborn, Michigan, August 6, 1921 — Single Copy Ten Cents

And Now Leprosy Is Yielding to Science
Years of experimenting brings a remedy

Fountain Lake, the Home of John Muir
A story of naturalist's wilderness abode

Fighting the Devil in Modern Babylon
First of a series of articles on New York by Rev. Dr. John Roach Straton

Jewish Jazz—Moron Music—Becomes Our National Music
Story of "Popular Song" Control in the United States

The Chief Justices of the Supreme Court
Only ten men have held this post since the tribunal was first organized

Teaching the Deaf to Hear With Their Eyes
How Chicago is educating afflicted children

Many By-Products From Sweet Potatoes
Recent discoveries prove great possibilities

The *Dearborn Independent*

Ford chose not to buy a well-known national paper. Instead, he bought his own small-town, local newspaper, the *Dearborn Independent*, which was read by people in Dearborn, but elsewhere was unheard of. Ford's ambitious plan was to make it into a major newspaper which would be read from coast to coast across America.

Through his paper he would 'speak' to the people of America. He would write about the things he believed in – and as the owner of the paper he could print more or less anything he desired.

Some of the things he believed in were deeply offensive. In 1920 the paper printed a front-page article with the headline: 'The International Jew: The World's Problem'. For the next 91 weeks the *Dearborn Independent* printed a stream of anti-Jewish stories, saying that problems in society were caused by the Jews. Henry Ford's **extremist views** exposed him as a **racist**. At the same time, Jews were working for him in his car factories.

An end to Ford's lies – and his paper

In 1924, the *Dearborn Independent* printed a story attacking a Jewish lawyer called Aaron Sapiro. The paper said Sapiro had cheated farmers out of a lot of money – which was untrue. Sapiro took the paper, and its owner Henry Ford, to court. But the case never got that far, because in 1927 Ford apologized to Sapiro and to all Jewish people. His apology was printed in his own newspaper. Ford's reputation had been damaged because of his outspoken beliefs, and his days as a newspaper owner were coming to an end. At the close of 1927 he shut down the *Dearborn Independent*.

A Life on View

Henry Ford lived much of his life in full view of the public. His cars made him a household name; people queued to work in his car factories; he was involved in **politics**; and, rightly or wrongly, he made his beliefs known through his newspaper. But there was so much more to Ford than most people could possibly know.

Henry Ford – philanthropist

As America's richest man, Henry could afford to be generous. Rather than donate a large sum of money and expect people to use it wisely, Ford wanted to make sure it was used the way he thought best. A good example of this is in Inkster, a small town near Detroit where people lived in poor conditions. Many were African-American, and many worked at Ford's car factories.

In 1931, Ford set up a supermarket in Inkster (one of the first in America), where people could buy low-priced food and clothing. He reopened the town school, gave seeds so people could grow flowers and vegetables in their gardens, bought sewing machines for the women, and provided lessons in dressmaking. Ford paid for the town's **electricity** supply. His generosity turned Inkster into a better, happier place, and he hoped his efforts would be an example to other run-down communities in America.

In 1919 Ford donated $11 million to set up a hospital, named after him, in Detroit. He said that, no matter whether a person was a prince or a pauper, they should be given an equal standard of care. Then in 1936, the Ford family set up the Ford Foundation, a charitable organization that provides money for research and education.

While Henry Ford became involved with politics and philanthropy, his car company was still building on its early successes.

The private life of Henry Ford

Some matters in Ford's life are shrouded in mystery. In 1923, at the Henry Ford Hospital, a typist at the Ford Motor Company gave birth to baby boy. Henry Ford took a special interest in this particular new arrival. A rumour spread that he was the child's father, but one thing is certain: Ford saw that the boy's family was well cared for and gave them land and a fine home, and there were always presents for the child.

Final Years

Edsel Ford was the natural – and only – choice to take over as president of the Ford Motor Company, which the Ford family owned outright. In 1919, when Edsel was only 25, Henry stood down, and Edsel took his place.

Time away from cars

Ford had no plans to disappear quietly into retirement and old age – far from it. He liked walking in the woods at Dearborn, bird-watching and collecting antiques – and became so keen on square dancing that he even employed a full-time dance instructor and a band – but his energy for new ideas never left him, and in his final years his mind turned to the past.

Edsel Bryant Ford (1893–1943)

Edsel was Henry and Clara Ford's only child. He grew up surrounded by his father's interest in cars, and was given his first car when he was only eight. There was no such thing as a minimum driving age then, and young Edsel drove himself to and from school. Edsel married Ellie Clay in 1916. Their eldest son, born the following year, was named Henry Ford II.

A museum at Dearborn

One of Ford's all-time heroes was Thomas Edison, his former employer. In the 1920s and 1930s Ford built a vast museum at Dearborn, named the Edison Institute of Technology in honour of the inventor to whom Ford said he owed so much. The idea was simple. Ford wanted the museum to show people 'what really happened in years gone by'. Ford bought and moved old buildings to his museum from all over America – and from England too. He moved a shepherd's cottage stone by stone across the Atlantic from there, and rebuilt it at Dearborn to show people the sort of humble dwelling their English ancestors might have lived in. From the towns and villages of America came old log cabins, inns, a blacksmith's forge, the courthouse where Abraham Lincoln had practised law, the buildings in which Edison had worked, and even a house where **electric** light had first been used.

Ford wanted the museum to tell his own story too, where children could learn about and experience the things he had done as a child, such as spinning wool, tending to crops, and caring for farm animals. Ford believed it was simple tasks like these that had made him the person he was.

Henry Ford (left) and Thomas Edison laying the corner stone of the Edison Institute of Technology (later renamed the Henry Ford Museum) in 1929.

The Legacy of Henry Ford

In 1943, Edsel Ford died from cancer at the early age of 49. Henry was then aged 80 and, despite being in poor health, he took charge of the company once more. It remained his wish that there should always be a member of the Ford family to lead the business, so in 1945 he handed control of the Ford Motor Company to his grandson, Henry Ford II (1917-87).

The Edsel, launched in 1957, was a medium-priced car with a high vertical radiator grille, which the public apparently didn't like. The Edsel lost the Ford Motor Company $250 million before production was stopped in 1959.

Henry Ford dies

Henry Ford died on Monday, 7 April 1947, aged 83, at his Dearborn home, Fair Lane, on a night when the Rouge River had burst its banks and flooded the cellars of the house. All **electric** power had been cut off, and the vast house was lit by candles. Ford had lived through the birth of the car, the aeroplane, electric light and the atomic bomb. Yet, on this night of all nights, it wasn't just Henry's life that stopped – it was as if time itself had stopped, recalling simpler days when homes were lit with lamps and candles, a time when '**automotive transportation**' was just a dream.

A modern Ford car plant, in Valencia, Spain.

Henry Ford's legacy

The company formed by Henry Ford in 1903 has grown into an international business success, with over 250 million Ford vehicles built to date. Ideas developed by Ford, especially to do with **mass production**, are now used by car factories worldwide. Although computerized machines do much of the work that in Ford's time was done by people, these factories all use his **moving assembly-line** process.

The Ford Motor Company today

In 1999, the Ford Motor Company was the world's second largest manufacturer of cars and trucks. It employed nearly 400,000 employees in over 20 countries. Henry Ford was named 'Businessman of the Century' by *Fortune*, an influential American business magazine, and the Model T was voted 'Car of the Century'. Car enthusiasts from around the world joined in the voting via the Internet, which Ford's current chairman, William Clay Ford, Jr, believes 'will be the moving assembly line of the 21st century'.

The Changing View of Henry Ford

It is the work of historians to tell the truth about the past. But finding out the truth can often be a difficult process.

> 'I am going to see that no man comes to know me.'
>
> Henry Ford

Henry Ford – his own words

The story of Ford's early life was published in 1922 in an 'autobiography' (written by a journalist, not by Ford) called *My Life and Work*. It became a bestseller. In it, some of the facts of Ford's life were changed. For example, Ford claimed that as a boy he had a workbench in his bedroom where he repaired watches for his neighbours – which his father had forbidden him to do. Ford said he would sneak from the house late at night, ride off on horseback to collect a watch, then repair it at his workbench. He wanted people to think he had fought against authority all his life. But Ford's sister, Margaret, remembers it differently. She said: 'Father never forbade him to repair neighbours' watches. I never knew of him going out at night to get watches ... there was nothing upstairs [in his bedroom] except his dresser and a little stand that he kept trinkets in, and his bed.'

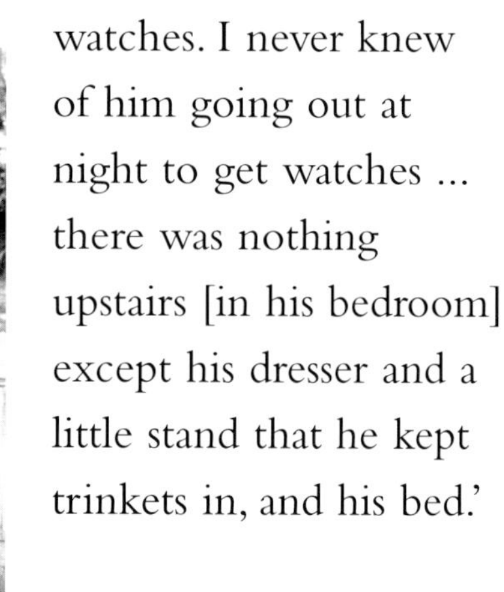

Henry and Clara with their grandson Henry Ford II at the Henry Ford Museum, Greenfield Village, in 1945.

Henry Ford – the words of others

In 1977, American writer James Brough wrote *The Ford Dynasty*. His book **depicted** Ford as a 'merciless employer who seldom stuck to his word', but who was also an 'authentic American **genius** whose **assembly-line** techniques revolutionized the world'. In 1986, British writer Robert Lacey wrote *Ford – The Men and the Machine*, which describes in great detail how Henry Ford had risen from farmboy to all-American folk hero.

By presenting the evidence, readers are left to draw their own conclusions about Henry Ford. As his success as a businessman increased, he became involved with **political** and social issues of the day, on which he held strong and often misguided views – he was, perhaps, a flawed genius. He was a tough man to work for, but was an enlightened employer who gave jobs to men and women regardless of their race or religion. He banned smoking in his factories and was one of the first employers to take on disabled people, whom other employers discriminated against. From reading all the sources on Henry Ford, one thing is crystal clear: he was a man with a vision of the future. His vision is today's real world in which the motor car is part of our everyday lives.

> 'You cannot learn in any school what the world is going to do next year.'
> Henry Ford

Henry Ford – Timeline

1863	Henry Ford was born on 30 July, to William Ford and Mary Litogot Ford, in Dearborn, Michigan
1876	Ford's mother dies. He sees a steam engine travelling along a road, and his fascination with machines begins.
1879	Ford leaves the family farm and goes to Detroit to work in the city's machine shops
1882	He returns home as an engineer, and makes plans for his future
1886	His father gives him land on which to build his own farm
1888	Marries Clara Bryant, of Greenfield township. They live on Henry's 80-acre farm.
1891	Returns to Detroit to work as an engineer with the Edison Illuminating Company
1893	Edsel Bryant Ford, only child of Henry and Clara Ford, is born
1896	Completes his first car, the Quadricycle, and drives it through the streets of Detroit
1899	Leaves the Edison Illuminating Company to begin a new career making cars. Made chief engineer and partner in the newly formed Detroit Automobile Company.
1900	The Detroit Automobile Company closes
1901	Helps form a new car-making company – the Henry Ford Company
1902	Leaves the Henry Ford Company, which changes its name to the Cadillac Automobile Company
1903	Helps form another company – the Ford Motor Company. The company's first car, the Ford Model A, is produced.

1908 Begins making the famous Ford Model T

1910 A new factory opens, at Highland Park, Detroit. It is designed for mass production.

1911 First overseas Ford car factory established, at Trafford Park, Manchester, England

1913 Introduces the first moving assembly line, at his Highland Park factory

1914 Pays male factory workers $5 for an eight-hour day (female workers did not receive this rate until 1916)

1915 The *King Oscar II*, Ford's 'Peace Ship', sails to Norway on a pacifist mission to end the First World War. The one millionth Ford car produced.

1918 Fails in his attempt to become elected to the US Senate. Buys the *Dearborn Independent* newspaper.

1919 Ford stands down from leading the Ford Motor Company. His son, Edsel, becomes the company's new president.

1927 Production of the Ford Model T ends. The *Dearborn Independent* prints an apology from Henry Ford about his views on Jews. The paper closes down.

1929 Opens the Edison Institute of Technology, a major museum

1936 Henry and Edsel Ford set up the Ford Foundation, a charitable organization

1943 Edsel Ford dies of cancer. Henry Ford resumes control of the Ford Motor Company.

1945 Henry Ford II takes charge of the Ford Motor Company

1947 Henry Ford dies, aged 83, at Fair Lane, his Dearborn home

1999 *Fortune* magazine names Henry Ford 'Businessman of the Century'. The Model T is named 'Car of the Century'.

Glossary

American Civil War (1861-65) fought between the northern and southern states of the USA
apprentice a person who is trained by an employer to do a job
assembly line where goods are assembled in a certain order by workers or machines
astute clever, but crafty, good at predicting business developments for own profit
automated a process in which goods are put together by machines
automobile a motor car
automotive transportation any type of vehicle which moves along using its own power
backer someone who supports (backs) another person, usually by providing them with money
chassis the metal base-frame of a car, to which all the other parts are attached
conveyor belt a wide belt which moves (conveys) goods
cylinder a part inside a car engine
depict to show, by means of a picture, or in words
designer someone who decides how a car should look, inside and outside
destiny someone's future, often out of their control
draft dodging American term meaning to avoid (dodge) military service if drafted (called) to join the army, navy or air force
election campaign the time immediately before an election when politicians try to persuade voters to elect them
electricity the power or energy used to give light and heat and work machines
emigrate to leave one country in order to settle in another country
engineer someone who makes machines, or who plans the building of roads and bridges
era period of history
experimental vehicle one built to try out new ideas
extremist views beliefs which most people disagree with
First World War the European war (1914–1918) in which America fought from 1917
fledgling newly created (hatched), but often used to describe a new industry
fuel supply the circulation of fuel inside a car engine
genius a gifted, very clever person
horseless carriages early road vehicles which moved without being pulled by horses

industrialization the process in which a country changes over from an economy based on farming to one based on factories and machinery
internal combustion engine car engine in which fuel burns (combusts) inside the engine
manufacturing industry one which makes things, from needles and pins to cars and computers
mass production the process in which huge numbers of identical things are made quickly and cheaply
mechanism the parts of a machine
milestone significant event
motor car industry name for the worldwide business that makes cars
moving assembly line where parts are moved along a line of workers or machines by conveyor belts
nationalism a movement that supports national independence
output how many things a business makes
partnership an agreement between two or more people to work together
philanthropist someone who helps others out of kindness
politics to do with the control and government of a country
publicity something that brings a matter to the attention of the public, for example a news item
racist someone who treats other people unfairly because they belong to a different race (group) of people
registered when something is officially written down for legal purposes
Senate in the United States, the Senate is the upper assembly of those who govern the nation. It has 100 members (two senators from each state) who are elected by the voters. Senate means 'council of elders' and US senators must be at least 30 years old.
steam engine an engine powered by steam
steel a strong metal made from iron
steering tiller early cars used tillers (like on boats) to steer them. Tillers were eventually replaced by steering wheels.
technology the study and use of machinery
transformed when something is changed from one thing to another
vanadium steel a type of lightweight steel
war effort when people work to make or grow things to help their country during a war
wrench a tool used for gripping and turning metal nuts (a spanner)

Index